My Teacher Doesn't Like Me

Dr. Percy Bland Sr.

Creative Touch Publishing LLC.

P.O. Box 7482
Warner Robins, GA 31095
ctpublishing14@gmail.com

Printed and bound in the United States of America

1. Educational. 2. Motivational. 3. Non-Fiction.

International Standard Book Number
978-0-578-32378-7

⟳ TABLE OF CONTENTS ⟲

⇒ MEET THE AUTHOR ⇐

Born into a family of educators in the 1950s in Arkansas, Dr. Percy Bland Sr. has been associated with the noble teaching profession for over 40 years. He earned his Bachelor's and Master's from Arkansas State University and his Doctorate in Educational Leadership from Immaculata University.

Dr. Bland is a motivational speaker and has done educational consulting throughout North America, Australia, and Asia.

During his professional career, he has been privileged to touch the lives of countless students from elementary school to graduate school, though there is one sentence that has always made him feel disheartened and dismayed: "My teacher doesn't like me."

Join Dr. Bland as he candidly shares his most significant educational experiences and delves a little deeper into one of the most common perceptions among students of all ages, genders, races, and economic backgrounds.

⊳ **DEDICATION** ⊲

To my Lord and Savior Jesus Christ, without You, I can do nothing.

My deepest love and gratitude belong to my wife and best friend, LaFaye, to whom I dedicate this book. All that I have achieved and all that I have become are a direct result of your infinite love and support.

To my three children, Raea, Kelly, and Percy Jr., my grandchildren EVon, Elijah, Andrew, Josiah, Joshua, Kaeden, Caleb, and Eason, who provided their constant love, tolerance, and support as I wrote this book.

ACKNOWLEDGEMENTS

I'm especially grateful to honor my parents, grandparents and great grandparents, who were my first teachers. They are acknowledged for instilling in me the love and value of teaching and learning. They are namely:

- Parents: My father, Edgar Bland, Sr., who was a high school English teacher for 35 years. My mother, Etta Jescena Edmonson Bland, who was my third-grade teacher and an Elementary and Special Ed. teacher for 49 years.
- My maternal grandparents, James Edmonson Sr., my first principal, and Miriam Nero Edmonson, a home economics teacher.
- My maternal great-grandparents, S.T Nero and Etta Smith Nero, who were both teachers.
- My brothers, Vandell, Edgar Jr., Byron, and my sister, Jescena, for their constant love, support, encouragement, and optimism.
- My cousin, John Ann Riley, thank you for your constant love, support, and encouragement during the writing and completion of this book.

A special thanks to my former professor Dr. Larry Chapman, and my former graduate professor, colleague, and mentor Dr. George Eves.

I would also like to thank every teacher I've ever had from first grade to graduate school, and all of my past students who made my educational career a wonderful experience.

Thank you to all who have supported my efforts in accomplishing the writing of this book.

$\triangleright$ **INTRODUCTION** $\triangleleft$

I am tremendously grateful for the opportunity to share some of my educational experiences in this book. Collectively, my career consisted of thirty-four years as an elementary and high school teacher, an administrator, and both an undergraduate and graduate school professor.

I was fortunate enough to teach and touch students' lives at each grade level, from first grade to graduate school. Unfortunately, one phrase I have never been thrilled to hear was, "my teacher doesn't like me." I believe these words have been recited by almost every person who has ever attended any school, whether public or private.

For over thirty-four years as an educator, I have often pondered why this phrase has been so prevalent among students. Having been a student, an educator, and a parent, I have seen first-hand the devastating impact this belief—that their teacher dislikes them— has on a student. Believing they are opposed by their teacher has a negative effect on students as well their parents.

I've written this book to encourage all parties who have ever been affected by the phrase, "my teacher doesn't like me." Although I believe this does occur, I certainly hope that it is more of a misunderstanding or miscommunication on either the student or the teacher. This book was written with the intent of enlightening students, teachers, administrators, and parents. My goal is to help all involved parties understand each other and to work toward a common goal, which is for learning to occur inside the classroom.

It serves as a reminder that all stakeholders, students, parents, grandparents, teachers, and administrators have far too much to lose by allowing this phrase to continue to be internalized by millions of students. Unfortunately, too many students have been discouraged and given up hope in schools because they assumed that a teacher or an administrator did not like them. This book will investigate why students believe this to be true and explore different ways to address these issues. When students believe a teacher doesn't like them, it impedes learning. When and wherever learning is impeded, all involved parties suffer. Whatever perceptions held by either the student or the teacher has to be closely examined immediately. I believe it is incumbent upon educators to change this perception.

If this is a student's perception, educators must address it because perception is TRUTH, as I'll discuss shortly. Teachers must always utilize all available resources, services, and techniques available to them to reach students who may appear to be indifferent toward learning in their classroom. With the implementation of these appropriate teacher interventions, the likelihood of changing perceptions that may impede learning is great. This practice will eliminate all emotional obstacles that often preclude teaching and learning. Once this is done, the door swings open for optimal learning.

CHAPTER ONE

Teaching is a Calling

The value of a teacher is priceless. I know of no other profession that is nobler. Teachers have been the backbone of this world in our society since the inception of time. The concept of transmitting knowledge is valuable in every aspect of life.

Everyone has been a teacher and a student at some point during their lifetime. Both teaching and learning begin from the moment a child enters the world. If you are a parent, you have been entrusted with teaching your child how to navigate through a complex society and achieve their dreams.

Parents are also expected to responsibly teach specific values to their children, such as being courteous, grateful, honest, and respectful. These principles are priceless and are often learned before formal schooling. The unique thing about teaching and learning is that it occurs unintentionally and intentionally. Although learning happens unintentionally, effective teaching is accomplished with careful planning, implementation, and an applicable evaluation of your particular goals.

There are some in the teaching profession who are CALLED to teach. These individuals have the uncanny ability to bring clarity to whatever is being taught. A calling to teach is usually accompanied by a sincere love for all students, the gift of patience, and a passion for teaching and reaching. Love, patience, and passion cannot be learned from teacher education programs. Sometimes people believe that they are able to teach simply because they have attended school as a student.

Not everyone standing in front of a classroom can deliver instruction with lucidity. Some aspects of teaching, such as creating an emotionally safe environment, gaining the trust and respect of your students, and making each student feel a part of the classroom, are needed to maximize student learning. If you, as a teacher, are overlooking any of these elements, some students may have already internalized that their teacher does not like them.

Many teachers are very knowledgeable of their content but may overlook one of these elements and possibly minimize the learning experience for one or more students. Sitting on one side of the desk as a student is entirely different from sitting on the other side of the desk as a teacher. Some of the best athletes have experienced great difficulty in coaching the sport they mastered as a player.

Why Do People Choose to Become Teachers?

Those who choose teaching as a career are sometimes inspired by former teachers they admire. Some schools have organizations such as FTA (Future Teachers of America) that students join because teachers believe these individuals possess the unique ability to evolve into effective educators. Meanwhile, some have desired to teach from a very early age. Ultimately, teaching is a divine call to advance society, assist in shaping the future, and mold and nourish lives.

When someone is indeed called to be a teacher, any other profession they choose to enter will not entirely satisfy them. I've seen many graduate students go into teaching after receiving a bachelor's degree in another field. Many of my graduate students held degrees in disciplines other than education. Many professions are more lucrative than education, but very few are as intrinsically rewarding. Whatever career a person chooses, they should make sure they love it and enjoy it, almost to the point that they do it for free. A teacher who answers the call to teach satisfies an insatiable appetite that can't be soothed by money or fame. These teachers love all students, regardless of their sex, color, religion, or economic status.

Why is being called into this noble profession so imperative? Because every student that enters your classroom wants to believe that they are entering an emotionally safe environment. Additionally, all parents initially want to believe in teachers and that their child is in a teacher's classroom that is passionate about teaching, loves students, and has their child's welfare at the forefront. Teachers who are called will always ensure that all students feel safe. They create an environment conducive to learning.

The Pressures on Teachers

Teachers sometimes feel pressured to finish the course or book, so they believe they have only minimal time to spend on each chapter. Unfortunately, this leaves some students at a disadvantage, especially in disciplines such as math, where the mastery of certain concepts is imperative before proceeding to the following concept.

For example, if you don't master addition, subtraction, and multiplication, you will not learn division. Moreover, what about those students who get lost in the shuffle? What happens to the shy child who didn't want to draw attention to himself by asking questions, even though he didn't comprehend what was being taught for the past couple of weeks?

Since teaching and learning occur non-verbally just as frequently as verbally, teachers can employ non-verbal options to initiate dialogues with such students. Instead of asking shy children to raise their hands in class or participate in activities that may worsen their anxiety, educators must show compassion and understanding to create a safe and healthy environment.

For example, by asking each student to write the answer on a piece of paper as the teacher peruses the classroom and makes mental notes of the students with incorrect answers so the appropriate remediation can safely take place without any humiliation. Other tried and tested methods must also be implemented to access student comprehension without the risk of embarrassing such students.

Changing Perception

After a student fails a couple of tests, many educators infer that they can't do the work and often begin focusing on other students. Consequently, many students come to the unfortunate conclusion that "my teacher doesn't like me." Meanwhile, periodic comprehension checks would have detected what concepts had not been mastered and provided the teacher with an opportunity for content remediation.

I've never spoken with anyone who hasn't uttered those words about at least one teacher they have had during their time in school. Are all of them true? I certainly have my doubts. But absolutely all of those perceptions are true. Perception is always the TRUTH!

Why? It is truly authentic because this is how students perceive things that they believe to be true. This is the challenge I had as an educator, and it is the challenge of every individual who is called to teach. I've had many students say that I didn't like them. Although I disagreed, it did not alter the perception they had formed. I was unable to negate their perception.

Children often say that their parents don't like them after being grounded or given an early curfew. Now, we know that any sane parent who loves their child(ren) makes them come home at a decent hour, especially at night, but that still doesn't change the child's perception. Eventually, the child grows older and acquires wisdom; the child understands that the parent has their safety or welfare at the forefront of their mind.

Teachers have to accept students' perceptions and find special strategies and teaching modalities that will allow them to eventually experience classroom success. This should always be followed with praise.

On the contrary, flunking one class to create a positive influence can turn students entirely off from that discipline for life. I've witnessed many students say "I'm not good at math" because of a bad experience they had with a teacher in elementary school. On average, early childhood and elementary teachers spend at least five hours a day with a student. That is enough time to influence children to become all they can be.

Children walk into schools at the age of five and leave as adults. As educators, we have the tremendous responsibility of helping productivity and shaping doctors, lawyers, teachers, pastors, businessmen and women, entrepreneurs, and other skilled and unskilled workers who help make up our society. One of the worst things that can happen in any child's life is to believe that their teacher does not like them, for whatever justification. I believe that it is often the child's perception, yet there have been times when I have heard teachers say that they do not like particular students.

Teachers often have no idea how a child is feeling and why that child responds so negatively toward them. A passionate teacher, however, will immediately investigate by reaching out to the parents, reading anecdotal notes from past teachers, and conference with the student.

A person indeed called to teach will never settle with any student feeling unloved, or insignificant. Just as most human beings, children want to feel loved, and they deserve to feel valued and relevant at home and school.

Possibly, one of the reasons gangs have grown and continue to prevail is because gang members so frequently haven't felt relevant in the classroom. Gang leaders tend to recruit individuals who feel rejected from school and society at large.

As a student, I had teachers who knew their content and delivered it expertly, but I could never connect with them emotionally. Unfortunately, I spent most of my middle and high school years believing I was irrelevant to the people in authority in the world of academia.

Teachers who are passionate about teaching not only lucidly deliver instruction but also remove all distractions. Called teachers do what they need to do for learning to take place. Sometimes this is misconstrued by students as well as parents. However, in the end, knowledge is disseminated, and the students feel good about school.

Questions teachers should ask themselves:

- What made me want to go into the teaching profession?

- Do I still have a passion for teaching?

- How can I reach all of my students?

CHAPTER TWO

The Learning Environment

Every child that enters your classroom, and their parents, want to believe that they are entering an emotionally safe environment. Teachers who are called help ensure that all students feel loved, respected, and secure. This is an environment conducive to learning.

I was born in Elaine, Arkansas, a small rural town approximately 90 miles south of Memphis, Tennessee. Being born in 1958, less than forty years after the infamous 1919 race riot in Elaine, there was still a profound fragrance of racial subservience. Most residents in this rural town lived below the poverty line. There was no free preschool or kindergarten, leaving most children with little or no educational exposure until first grade.

Although I was born into a family of educators, the Jim Crow laws were very much alive and invariably a part of our everyday life. The environment consistently reminded people of color of their second-class citizenship in "The South."

For example, my grandfather was the principal of the "Black school," which had no cafeteria and no team sports. On the contrary, our "White" counterparts had hot meals prepared daily in the cafeteria and indulged in various athletic activities.

Nonetheless, life was perfect because we were surrounded by adults who loved and nurtured us. Both my grandparents and parents lived on the school campus. While my grandfather was the principal, my grandmother, father, and mother were teachers in his building. These four adults were my first teachers before entering first grade. They always instilled in us the value of learning and getting an education.

As teachers, my parents and grandparents believed all children had value and were relevant, regardless of their race, religion, or socioeconomic status. They believed all students deserved to be loved, respected, and given a good education.

Although most of the students came from financially challenged families, our teachers worked relentlessly to ensure the environment was facilitative to learning. The teachers successfully encouraged all students to participate in class actions and engaged them in the learning activities. The teachers fostered a learning environment that encouraged comfortable academic competition that challenged and rewarded all partakers.

Our teachers in elementary school always gave us a sense of belonging inside the classroom. The classrooms were meticulously decorated with encouraging quotes on the walls and the bulletin board. Our small, segregated school had a communal atmosphere. The students felt that the teachers cared about them, which made them want to do well in school. The teachers led by example with respect and trust, and the students reciprocated. Today, many of those students are professionals and influential people, making significant contributions to society.

One of my best friends from first grade, Mr. Derome Bobo, recently retired as the second person in command for the United States Postal Service in Memphis, Tennessee. Derome said he attributes much of his success to the love, discipline, and teachings of the educators like my parents and grandparents.

The school was fun, and we believed our teachers loved us. They made learning fun, yet they had expectations that we all could and would succeed in their classes.

My mother was my third-grade teacher. Through her, I witnessed firsthand a teacher who taught every student as though they were her child. The parents were 100% supportive of the teachers because they recognized that they loved their children.

My childhood school days were blissful! I felt so surrounded by love from both the students and teachers.

The air was so fresh; each breeze gave me a sense of how much I was loved, and I wanted to be valued by the adult teachers who were educating me. We had so much fun on our school campus. There was a baseball field, outside basketball courts, a merry-go-round, a jungle gym, and see-saws on which we played. And because we lived on the campus, we had the added benefit of enjoying these amenities year-round.

Although the schools were segregated, and ours only had grades one through eight, my teachers taught us never to feel inferior to anyone. Once students completed eighth grade, they had to attend another school to finish high school. We were taught to love all people and never look down on anyone, regardless of how they looked. I was taught we can love everyone while at the same time disliking specific behaviors. I carried that sentiment with me throughout my teaching career.

The Jim Crow Laws precluded Blacks and Whites from attending the same school under the separate but equal ruling handed down from the Supreme Court in the 1896 Plessy vs. Ferguson case. The law handed down by the Supreme Court of the United States permitted schools to be separated by race as long as all things were equal. But, of course, things were not equal.

For example, the Black school I attended had no football team, no cafeteria, and the books we received were old and had previously been used at the White school. Imagine getting a history book that is ten years old. That was the separate but equal treatment children of color received during that era in the South. My teachers never focused on what they did not have or the overt racial inequities. Instead, they became creative and utilized whatever resources were available to educate us properly. I was very blessed to have come from a family of educators. Because my parents and grandparents were college-educated, I was exposed to the joy of learning from birth, and I entered first grade at the age of four.

Most of my elementary school teachers connected learning with the relevance of learning and made us aware of its application to everyday life. My teachers strategically ascertained that their students were emotionally invested in the learning process. I vividly remember how my teachers wanted every student to enjoy the learning process. Whatever we were learning, each student had an opportunity of having the lead role. All students felt equally important daily. They assured us that we would not be disappointed in the end.

During that era, teachers of color, including my parents and grandparents, were acutely aware of how so many things could be taken away from them. Hence, they constantly told us, "Get an education because that is something that no one will ever be able to take away from you." They engineered an environment that made us want to learn because the knowledge would be with us for a lifetime.

Getting an education was not optional. I count myself truly blessed to have had so many role models and childhood heroes right in my own family. The inequalities were quite overt, but that was never used as a crutch for not giving your best effort in every situation. During grades one through sixth, I received a confluent education, one filled with the rigor that stimulated both the cognitive and affective domains.

A good education addresses both the cognitive and affective domains. Sometimes the affective aspect of teaching is left out of the planning. It refers to the tracking of growth in feelings or volatile areas during the learning process. All students are not the same and our lesson plans should reflect it. Students learn differently and have different emotional needs. Sometimes a brief conversation with a student is all that is needed to reach them. A teacher should involve the students' feelings, emotions, and attitudes in their planning.

Content Relevance

Content relevance is a very important aspect of the cognitive domain. Connecting relevance to new learning is always practical when introducing new content. To show content relevance is to illustrate why or how you will need this content in the future. Teachers should embrace students who ask why they need to learn certain concepts, rather than simply answering "because it's on the test."

Passionate teachers that are called to teach know how to bring the content to life and show its relevance by helping students discover how practical all knowledge can be. Content relevance refers to a student's perceptions of how course content may address their interests, needs, and goals. Teachers can help students realize that what they learn in class is exciting and worth knowing.

Educators often neglect to connect the content with real-life experiences or don't take the time to ensure that all their students can make that real-life connection, which often results in cramming.

Granted, most students can survive their classes by cramming the information and regurgitating the content back to the teacher on the day of the test, but this method of teaching and learning is often short-lived and reduces the overall potential of students.

Moreover, trying to cram too much information in a short period typically leads to lowered comprehension and poor performance. On the other hand, establishing content relevance helps students retain essential information even after the test time.

My younger brother, Dr. Byron Bland, had an elementary school reading teacher named Mrs. Hammonds. She was an excellent teacher and always told her students, "Learn to read and read to learn." Wow! What a way to show relevance.

Connecting new learning to relevance isn't optional. Mrs. Hammonds' sayings and her love of teaching others how to read had such a profound effect on my brother that he went on to get his doctorate degree in reading.

After becoming a college professor, he often spoke of Mrs. Hammonds' class and her influence on his life. There were many times while traveling Dr. Bland would read signs on the road and comment, "If it had not been for Mrs. Hammonds' reading class, I would not know how to navigate through this city."

If learning is absent, there is no teaching. Teaching with relevance coupled with an emotionally safe environment makes learning fun.

Mrs. Barney, my fourth-grade social studies teacher, had a lasting effect on my life. She was the only teacher at my elementary school that I don't ever recall seeing with a smile. She appeared unhappy most of the time. In class, she never smiled at me or cordially spoke to me. I worked hard and did the best I could in her class but always fell short of making an A or B. It was apparent because I made A's and B's in my other classes.

For the first time, I uttered these words to my parents, "My Teacher Doesn't Like Me."

As a seven-year-old, it was the first time I can remember feeling that a teacher didn't like me. Because I was two years younger than everyone else in my class, I was very shy and reserved. I tried to be the best student I could be in all of my classes, but regardless of how hard I worked, somehow, my best just wasn't good enough for Mrs. Barney. She never called on me to help in any way, nor did she ever give me, a fourth grader, any complement on my class work.

One marking period I was devastated when I saw a "D" on my report card. During first through third grades, the lowest grade I had ever received was a "B". So, receiving a "D" left me confused. What am I going to tell my parents? Should I run away? If they had known, my parents would have tutored me. My parents worked on the same faculty, and they would've been extremely grateful to have gotten a heads up on my academic performance to have the opportunity to remediate me.

I shut down and closed the shop. I became even more reserved in her class and eventually believed it didn't matter how hard I tried; I could not do well in social studies. It was my perception that Mrs. Barney did not like me. I also believed that her expectations of me succeeding in her class were very low.

Unfortunately, that attitude stayed with me throughout the rest of elementary school, secondary school, and even college. I always had the thought, "I don't do well in social studies." I never knew or understood the impact Mrs. Barney had on my life after fourth grade.

It is essential to understand that all teachers bring something into your life that makes you a better person. My experience with Mrs. Barney made me particularly sensitive toward shy students when I became a teacher. I tried not to give any student the perception that I did not like them. Although I was not particularly happy during the time I was in her class, I now realize that I needed a Mrs. Barney in my life to help make me the educator that I was fortunate enough to become.

The Impact on Underprivileged Children

The learning environment is critical when it comes to teaching and learning. Unfortunately, many children from rural areas and inner cities have been economically deprived for many generations. When a child is born in an underprivileged family, it is almost certain that they will experience academic deficiencies before entering the public school system.

These students are often provided with a watered-down curriculum that deprives them of the opportunity to catch up with their peers. Many kindergartners are disadvantaged from day one because they have been in a poor environment that has stifled much of their learning. A family's economic status is the number one indicator of academic success.

Regardless, a concerned and loving teacher can engineer an environment that can certainly accelerate learning for disadvantaged students.

An Emotionally Safe Environment

Creating an emotionally safe environment, coupled with teaching with relevance, is paramount to learning. It is the responsibility of the teacher to create a loving and trusting environment so that their students feel valued and emotionally safe while in their classroom. As an educator, my goal was always to gain students' respect by giving respect. I found this to be confirmed on every level, from elementary to graduate school. A simple smile as a student enters your classroom can positively affect how they are willing to learn from you.

Students are very good at knowing when they are loved by someone. If they don't feel loved and safe in a teaching environment, learning will be affected. On the contrary, when they feel safe, they open their hearts and their minds.

Parents believe that all teachers will genuinely help their children learn and become successful, contributing members of society. Nevertheless, learning is so much easier when the students believe they are loved, wanted, and valued.

Unfortunately, many students attend school every day believing that their teachers do not want or love them. The perception of students being disliked by a teacher can be eradicated by simply creating a learning environment for all students. After all, every student deserves to feel loved, trusted, and respected by their mentors.

We all remember teachers who were firm but fair, loving, and caring. Once students believe a teacher likes them, they will diligently perform in that teacher's class. Students look forward to attending those classes because of the safe learning environment and their teacher's passion for teaching the subject matter. Parents want to believe that all teachers have the passion to see children learn.

I believe most teachers do, particularly those that are called. Students that may not talk much at school but are not limited to being very verbally open at home usually have something in common. At home, they feel safe; that is, they believe they are around people who love them, value them, and want them to succeed.

Questions Teachers Should Ask Themselves:

- What strategies do I employ to help students feel safe?

- What am I doing to help economically disadvantaged students have the same opportunities as their counterparts?

- How can I show more contact relevance in my teaching?

A picture of the Elaine Jr. High School faculty in the late 1960s. My grandfather (principal) and grandmother are in the second row, third and fourth from the far left. My father, Mr. Edgar Bland, Sr., is on the far right of the third row

My grandfather, Mr. James Edmonson

A photograph of my mother, Etta Jescena Edmonson Bland, along with a newspaper article in which she is featured as 1974 Arkansas Special Ed. Teacher of the Year

$\succ$ CHAPTER THREE $\prec$

Culture Shock

After completing elementary school, my parents moved to Helena, Arkansas, approximately twenty-five miles north of Elaine, Arkansas. After the move to Helena, my parents placed us in an integrated school under the "Freedom of Choice" law, which had been in effect for approximately three years.

My parents, being educators, still had minor concerns about sending my older brother and me to this newly integrated school, especially since everything was still relatively unfamiliar to us, even in our community. After much deliberation, my parents sent my older brother and me to the new "White school."

Many Black parents opted to keep their children in the Black school. Many of them were nervous about the type of treatment their children would receive from the White teachers. Because I had entered first grade at the age of four, I entered my new school in the seventh grade at the age of ten. I remember being nervous but trying not to show it every day. This had a major impact on my academic success. I never mentioned that I was two years younger than my peers, and I tried to satisfy everyone. I missed my old school and old friends, but I wanted to show my parents that I could handle the move. Needless to say, because of the Jim Crow laws, I'd never had any substantial interactions with White people. I was preoccupied daily as I tried to comprehend and conquer this new culture shock.

The New School

I spent hours upon hours looking at the outer differences between the White teachers, students, and me. I remember being very frightened and intimidated, which led me into a state of isolation. The teachers didn't seem even to notice that I was part of their classes. I never had one single conversation with a teacher, inside or outside of the classroom. As I reflect, I have often wondered why some adults did not notice my state of isolation and attempt to; even superficially, engage in a conversation with me. Most days I walked around alone and in fear. Emotionally, I always felt that I was seconds from crying.

I often refer to grades seven through twelve as my "years of obscurity." During those years, I was extremely removed from the academic arena. The six years of secondary school passed very slowly. My life was filled with fear as I scrambled to find meaning for my existence. I entered seventh grade at ten and turned sixteen just before graduating high school.

Beforehand, I recall being so excited about the possibility of attending this new school, and after ultimately getting there, I felt grossly misplaced, excluded, and unwanted. I was always in a state of seclusion. No one asked if I wanted to sit with them in the cafeteria, and in my classrooms, I usually sat next to someone who rarely spoke to me. Why didn't some teacher or adult come to my rescue? In my old school, teachers that did not even teach me would strike up a conversation with you. They knew who you were, as well as who your friends were.

Because of the prior segregation laws, I believe my counterparts were just as reluctant to be around me as I was to be in their presence. Society had somehow placed an unfair barrier between us to make us feel differently because of the colors of our skin. Interestingly, it is a reluctance I still see even today.

Experiences like these helped me shape my feelings about that "isolated student" during my teaching career. Each year, I sought out that "isolated student" and made it my goal to integrate them into every activity possible to eradicate the isolation of any student. I never wanted any student to feel like I did in grades seven through twelve.

As a young student, I spent most of my time in class daydreaming. I recall leaving class and not remembering one thing the teacher said. I failed quiz after quiz and test after test. I was never called in to discuss a lousy test score by a teacher, a guidance counselor, or an administrator. I was ignored and emotionally abandoned by adults and never told what to do to get back on track. I was just left to myself to kind of "freelance."

The first marking period came to an end quickly, and I was caught off guard with my grades. For some odd reason, I thought that everything was okay because I had not been pulled aside by any teachers as I would have been in elementary school. During that marking period, I received all F's in the four major academic areas. This captured the genesis of my academic detachment.

Teacher-Parent Communication

I can only imagine what my parents thought once I took my report card home. They were accustomed to most of my teachers giving feedback to them about my academic progression or regression. In my old, racially segregated school, there was only one teacher, Mrs. Barney, who had neglected to communicate with my parents and me about my academic status. I later realized that she had unresolved issues with my grandfather, the principal, so she had decided to get revenge by ignoring his grandson. Mrs. Barney was the only teacher in elementary school that neglected to keep my parents abreast of my academic progress, even though their classrooms were only a few feet away.

Things were very different at my new school. Not one teacher contacted my parents or phoned them for any parental intervention due to my failing their classes. There was a total disconnect between the school and my teachers with my parents and me.

When I think about my middle and high school teachers, I can only imagine how much difficulty they may have had connecting with me also because they had been—at least some of them—educated twenty years earlier in the 1940s and 1950s. My teachers' professors could very well have been educated twenty or thirty years earlier. I'm almost sure that none of them ever dreamed of having a Black student, and therefore, this would have been entirely left out of any teacher education curriculum.

However, it does not matter what the student looks like; good teaching requires involvement with the parents.

So, we have teachers who were educated in the early'50s and taught by professors who were educated inthe '20s and '30s, attempting to teach students of a different race and culture in the 1960s.

There was no cultural congruity and no effort to try and understand my culture. When there is no effort to understand a different culture, it is always a lose-lose situation. I'm a great advocate of teachers returning to school to stay abreast of innovative ways to teach all students effectively.

Changes in society are constant, and the schools have to reflect those changes for optimal learning. Appropriate education will always address cultural differences and cultural learning styles.

Communication between home and school is essential for students to succeed academically. All parents, regardless of their race or economic status, want to see their children do well in school and life. It is incumbent upon the school to initiate correspondence with the parents if there is any real academic success experienced by the student.

Because the law requires student-athletes to maintain a certain grade point average to be eligible to participate in team sports, sometimes coaches tend to have more parental contact than academic teachers. However, even with some coaches, they will cease parental contact when their season is over. It's almost as though I care about your child as long as they can win for me.

As a 10-year-old 7th grader in a new environment, I did not have the self-advocacy skills to approach my teachers about my grades. What was somewhat questionable to my parents and me was that my teachers did not approach me or contact my parents concerning my academic regression. Had they reviewed my academic records from elementary school? A fifteen-minute investigation of my elementary records would have revealed everything about my academic potential. At no time should a student struggling academically continue to regress because there is no teacher/parent communication.

I was very fortunate that my parents, being educators, were able to adequately assess the situation, make appropriate adjustments, and develop a viable solution. Every child doesn't have such a great support system. My mother had a Master's Degree in Special Education and was very aware of individualized educational plans and academic remediation.

The very next marking period I was able to get back on the right track. Unfortunately, I was never that A/B student again, but I finished high school, mainly making C's and D's with an occasional B. Once I got to the 9th grade, I had a whole new set of values and ideologies about school and my teachers. I believed my teachers didn't like me, so I closed shop. Eventually, I even began to believe that I was incapable of attaining high academic achievement.

The Emotional Detachment

The emotional connection with my teachers was detached during the first marking period of my seventh-grade year and rapidly deteriorated over the next six years. The emotional divorce from the academic arena was so deep that my self-esteem was severely injured. I didn't believe I was capable of making good grades any longer. Just four months prior, I'd been an honor roll student, and now I was a D and F student? As a ten-year-old seventh grader, I concluded, "my teacher doesn't like me." Because of the minimized contact I had with my teachers, the physical and emotional connection that I'd once had in elementary school quickly dissipated.

During high school, I was very emotionally detached and therefore did not involve myself in many school activities. Other than playing basketball, I was utterly disconnected from high school in general. In my senior year, the detachment reached an all-time high, even to the point where I gave up the only sport I was involved in: basketball.

After this prolonged period of social and academic isolation, I sought happiness from peers as academically unhinged as myself. I was ceasing to function in school while simultaneously making the Dean's list on the streets.

Unfortunately, this kind of mental evacuation from the academic arena is incredibly prevalent among students who have been emotionally injured in school.

Indifferent attitudes toward learning can easily detect emotional detachment from school. Many prison inmates had experienced this same detachment or disconnection when they were students in school. I remain optimistic that teachers and administrators will begin considering these devastating effects on children and take proactive steps by initiating strategies to keep parents abreast of all social and academic changes with their children.

As a teacher, if you speculate that any of your students seem to be indifferent about school or learning in your class, you must find a way to let that student know three things:

- I see you.

- You are wanted and needed.
- You are capable of succeeding in my class and life in general.

Had these three concepts been utilized in every classroom in America for the past sixty years, the racial landscape of our prison populations would look substantially different.

Whether you are an administrator or a custodian, once you sense a disconnection between the school and a student, I encourage you to contact their teacher so that an effort can be made to ensure that the student feels like they are part of the school. All students want to feel welcomed and be reassured that they can succeed. Every adult who comes in contact with a student, from the bus driver to the principal, has the potential of being a change agent.

Children must believe that they are valued at home and school. It is important for parents to understand and share their child's perceptions of their teachers. I would advise parents to call for a parent-teacher meeting when their child exhibits signs of disliking their school. Resolving the issues of your child IS A MUST!

The teacher may be totally oblivious to the child's perception. Communication is vital when addressing a disconnection and eradicating feelings of alienation. Feel free to share what your child likes or dislikes. Also, be open to sharing their sensitivities. I have often said, "If a teacher finds the world the child lives in, he or she will find that student."

Joshua and Ms. Benson

Pictured here with my grandson Joshua is his fourth-grade teacher Ms. Benson, who took time out of her busy schedule, having two small children of her own, to come out on a Sunday night and watch one of Josh's basketball games. Ms. Benson realized that to effectively reach a slightly distracted academic student such as Joshua, it was imperative to enter his world, which consists of a deep love for basketballand football.

Because of Ms. Benson's extra effort to connect with Joshua, she has become a household name at his home. Not to mention that Joshua wants to do everything he can to succeed in her class. Learning becomes more accessible when a student believes a teacher loves them.

Questions teachers should ask themselves:

- What strategies do I use to include all children in learning activities?

- Do I communicate successfully with my students' parents?

- What steps can I take to connect with my students emotionally?

$\sum$ CHAPTER FOUR $\lessgtr$

A Reconnection to School

Students develop at different stages; physically, physiologically, and emotionally. I started first grade at the age of four. Academically, I was more than ready to take on any task put in front of me because of my loving and caring teachers. Owing to the racial ramifications from the Jim Crow Era, when I grew up, I became emotionally and psychologically disconnected from school after integration. As a seventh grader, I realized that my coping skills were less than the situational demands.

Leaving a sheltered environment after sixth grade and entering middle school, I quickly realized that I did not have the social skills necessary to integrate myself into a foreign environment appropriately. I was traumatized by the social alienation of my peers, teachers, and administrators. I could not self-integrate myself with my environment, even with people involved in the same activities.

This deficiency in self-advocacy caused me to receive failing grades and is one of many reasons why I held an indifferent attitude about learning from grades seven through twelve. I only wish I 'd had a teacher to pull me aside and find out why I was not performing in his or her grade. I don't think any of my teachers knew my young age. I was very self-conscious of my age and made sure that none of my friends knew my real age and no one found out. But it was public knowledge to any teacher and administrator who wanted to take the time to read my files or records.

Beginning in middle school, my experiences had not been excellent, and during my high school career, I had not detected any genuine love or care for me by any of my teachers. They lectured us and then left us to sink or swim. The teachers or administrators had no meetings with my parents from grades seven through twelve.

Choosing Your Destiny

After graduating from high school during the summer of 1974, I enrolled at Arkansas State University in the fall of that same year. After my acceptance into the university, I now had to declare a major. At the age of sixteen, I had no ambition and no real direction in life. At that time, I knew I did not want to be a teacher because everyone in my family was a teacher.

I recall having a good friend, Mr. Raymond Simes, majoring in radio and television. I thought, why not follow him? That day I became a radio and television major. Perfect, I will be on television, and I'll never have to be involved with teachers or school ever again. The first class I attended was Radio Basic Operations. That class was the longest fifty minutes of my life, and I absolutely hated every second of it. I hated it so much that immediately after class, I marched over to the administration building and dropped the course and the major. And what new major did I sign up for? You got it: Education.

I entered college to have as much fun as I possibly could. Because of the disconnection with school six years prior, I had no intention of becoming academically engaged any time soon. The first two years were introductory courses everyone had to enroll in before launching their substantial studies.

When I started taking education courses, I found them to be, much to my surprise, amazingly interesting. However, I still wasn't really emotionally invested in the field. Little did I know; teaching was my calling.

I always knew I wanted to teach teachers how to teach the "unteachable" and reach the "unreachable," but I never thought it would materialize traditionally. I now realize this desire was covertly birthed with my fourth-grade teacher, Mrs. Barney. That coupled with the fact that I had seen so many positive, loving, and caring teachers in elementary school, especially my parents and grandparents.

In the 70s, I did as many other college students did; I began experimenting with recreational drugs and alcohol. Although I was somewhat successful academically, my image as a hippie was not exactly inviting to some of my professors, mainly my advisor. I will call him Dr. Simron.

Dr. Simron relayed his dislike for me to one of my professors, Dr. Chapman, by asking him to fail me to get me expelled from the School of Education.

He stated to my professor that my image was not good for the school and that, in his professional opinion, I would never make a good teacher. I was acutely aware that Dr. Simron did not like me, but I had become acclimatized to teachers not liking me and went on about life.

Ironically, as my advisor, Dr. Simron was the one person that the university had designated to help me successfully navigate through school. What happens when your paid advocate gives up on you?

After receiving my Bachelor's degree, I completed my Master's the following year. I vividly remember sitting in the lobby of the education building one Saturday morning, about to take my comprehensive exam for my Master's Degree. Dr. Simron came out of his office, placed his hand on my shoulder, and stated, "Percy Bland, here you are about to get your Master's, and I never thought you would get your Bachelor's."

His plan to stop my calling was aborted, and because of Dr. Chapman, my teaching career divinely catapulted me into thirty-four wonderful years of "reaching and teaching" the disconnected.

A Great Teacher Can Change a Student's Life

Most people can remember a teacher they believed did not like them. On the contrary, most students can also remember a teacher they adored. Consequently, a more concentrated effort to succeed was made in that loved teacher's classroom. In my case, it was my professor, Dr. Larry Chapman. Although I never had Dr. Chapman as an undergraduate professor, whenever we saw each other, we always greeted each other with a smile. My hairstyle and unconventional way of dressing did not seem to bother him at all.

One day Dr. Chapman met with me and told me, word for word, what my advisor had asked him to do.

My advisor had asked Dr. Chapman to call me after finding out that I was enrolled in one of his classes. Dr. Chapman then said, "Percy, after hearing from your advisor, I made up my mind that you would get nothing less than a B in my class." This day marked a turning point for me. I thought, "Wow, someone does think I'm relevant."

Dr. Chapman had nothing to gain by telling me this. Little did he know just how profound and how life-changing this encounter was for me. I left that meeting with tears in my eyes, saying, "Wow, a teacher does care about me." I made up my mind that day that I was not only going to succeed in Dr. Chapman's class but also life.

After attending approximately six years of classes with teachers who showed no particular interest in me, I now found myself talking to someone who cared about me and believed in me. I didn't know it at the time, but I later realized that Dr. Chapman was God-sent. The conversation we'd had motivated me to prove that Dr. Simron was wrong. How dare he think I would not make a good teacher? Did he know me well enough to speak so negatively about my life? How did he have the audacity to judge my potential, my character, and my future as a teacher!

What gave him the right to speak so negatively about my chosen career path? Was it because of how I dressed, or perhaps because of my skin color? For a moment, I relived the resentment that had been internalized from my middle school and high school years. However, I was determined not to allow the sense of loneliness and alienation to take root in my mind to the point where I would throw my hands up and retreat to the streets. My school days of detachment were over!

I realized that Dr. Chapman saw worth in me. Behind the color of my skin and my hippie clothes, he saw worth. How many times do educators consciously or unconsciously throw students away because of how they look or dress? After that conversation with Dr. Chapman, *the entire trajectory of my life changed that day!*

I was motivated to prove to Dr. Chapman that his confidence in me would not be in vain. I was moved by his compassion and love for me. He was, in my opinion, what a real teacher should be required to do.

Any teacher can get a student to believe in them. But a teacher who is CALLED to teach gets the students to believe in themselves.

On that very day, I began to believe in myself. That was the day that becoming a teacher, a good caring teacher, became my passion. For a moment, I envisioned hundreds of future disconnected students in my classes being reconnected to school. Until that day, I believed that not one teacher, other than my parents and grandparents, really cared about my future. But this teacher, Dr. Larry Chapman, resurrected my faith in teachers and people in general.

On the other hand, I certainly do not want to underrate the effect that Dr. Simron had on my life.

He was a reminder of the type of teacher I NEVER wanted to become. He was the reason I wanted to teach teachers someday how to teach. I wonder if he ever suggested the idea of failing students who didn't fit their image of what an elementary or secondary student should look like, to any of his undergraduate students.

Sometimes, people come into our lives to show us what not to become. I believe that if my middle and high school teachers had articulated their belief in my academic abilities, I would have entered college with more confidence in my scholarly capabilities.

Without this negative incident with Dr. Simron, I'm not sure if my academic re-connections would have ever occurred. All things in your life seem to come back around for your good when you allow the negative things to encourage you to help others.

I had a former student who was well-behaved, but school just wasn't his niche. He decided that he was going to withdraw from school and attend a technical school full-time. His father was a businessman, and he wanted to prepare himself to take over the family business.

On the day he brought the withdrawal papers for me to sign, I asked, "What is the problem?" I told him if it were me, I'd switch him to another teacher's class. He then told me the reason for his withdrawal. I later learned that when he went to another teacher's class to get his signature to withdraw from the course, the teacher signed the paper, handed it back to him, and said, "Here you go, loser."

"Here you go, loser!" What a statement for a student to have to remember. This student shared his story with me twenty-five years after that episode. Although he is now the CEO of his own company, he never forgot the negative words spoken to him by this teacher. His determination to become successful was motivated by this teacher's negative outlook.

Teachers should never adopt the belief that just because some students are not doing well or are not academically inclined that they are somehow not pertinent to society. Just as I was motivated by Dr.

Simron's negative perception of me, my student was inspired by his teacher's negative perception of him.

I wish that this were always the case, but it's not. Some students have forever been marred and never been able to recover from the derogatory remarks made by their teachers.

Questions Teachers Should Ask Themselves:

- Are all of my students excited to come to my class?

- Am I pre-judging any of my students because of how they look?

- Is my relationship with my students hindering their ability to learn?

⇨ **CHAPTER FIVE** ⇦

Know Your Students

There are very few things concerning teaching that are more important than knowing your students. Assessing your student's academic potential is what we do as teachers. Another element of concern is knowing what your students' likes and dislikes are. For example, if you have a student that doesn't particularly like to read but loves basketball, center his assignments around anything concerning basketball.

Knowing who your students are will make challenging students less challenging. I've had my fair share of challenging students, both academically and socially. My professors did a great job preparing me on how to deliver content. The theory is good, but nothing compares to practice. If you are a brand-new teacher, I can guarantee you that you will encounter situations and circumstances about students that your professors did not teach you. Life is constantly changing, and one must be willing to change with society for learning to occur.

Most of my middle and high school teachers had never taught anyone who looked like me. When the law was changed, and integration took place, it was incumbent upon school districts to educate their teachers on cultural differences. The teacher education programs at universities also needed to modify their curriculum to address the learning styles of all students and cultural incongruencies.

Students' needs vary according to their individual learning styles. In today's public schools, students with learning disabilities are mainstreamed into traditional classes. Any curriculum that doesn't adequately address the cultural learning styles, as well as learning disabilities, doesn't   sufficiently address the educational needs of all students.

Some students are classified as homeless. Others have been emancipated for various reasons. Sometimes, a students' life outside the school can impede their academic performance. Hence, there is a real need for teachers to know who their students are to address their academic needs appropriately.

Teaching Graduate School

Fifteen of the best years of my life were spent educating teachers and administrators on effective ways to instruct the students that appear to be indifferent toward learning.

I had many experiences that helped me learn how to reach and teach students. However, I started the first day of each undergraduate and graduate class by sharing a story about Mrs. Thompson. I want to take a moment to share that story with you now.

This story originates many years ago and tells of an elementary school teacher named Mrs. Thompson. As she stood in front of her fifth-grade class on the first day of school, she told her students a lie.

Like most teachers, she looked at her students and told them that she loved them all the same. But that was not true because there in the front row, slumped in his seat, was a little boy named Teddy Stoddard.

Mrs. Thompson had watched Teddy the year before and noticed that he didn't play well with the other children. His clothes were messy and he always needed a bath. Moreover, Teddy could be unpleasant at times. It got to the point where Mrs. Thompson would take delight in marking his papers with a broad red pen. She would make bold Xs and finally put a Big "F" on the top of his writings.

At the school where Mrs. Thompson taught, she was required to review each child's records. She put Teddy's off till last. When she finally reviewed his file, she was in for a surprise.

Teddy's first-grade teacher wrote:
"Teddy is a bright child with a ready laugh. He does his work neatly and has good manners. He's a joy to be around."

His second-grade teacher wrote:
"Teddy is an excellent student and well-liked by his classmates. But he's troubled because his mother has a terminal illness, and life at home must be a struggle."

His third-grade teacher wrote:

"His mother's death has been hard on him. He tries to do his best, but his father doesn't show much interest. His home life will soon affect him if steps aren't taken."

Teddy's fourth-grade teacher wrote:

"Teddy is withdrawn and doesn't show much interest in school. He doesn't have many friends, and sometimes he even sleeps in class."

By now, Mrs. Thompson had realized the problem, and she was ashamed of herself. She felt even worse when her students brought her Christmas presents wrapped in beautiful ribbons and bright paper, except for Teddy's. His present was clumsily wrapped in heavy brown paper that he had gotten from a grocery bag. Mrs. Thompson took pains to open it in the middle of the other presents.

Some of the children started to laugh when she found a rhinestone bracelet with some of the stones missing and a bottle that was one-quarter full of perfume. But she stifled the children's laughter when she exclaimed how pretty the bracelet was while putting it on and then dabbing some of the perfume on her wrist.

Teddy Stoddard stayed after school that day just long enough to say, "Mrs. Thompson, today you smell just like my mom used to." After the children left, she cried for at least an hour.

On this very day, she quit teaching reading, writing, and arithmetic. Instead, she began to teach children. Mrs. Thompson started to pay close attention to Teddy as she worked with him. As time went on, his mind seemed to come alive. The more she encouraged him, the faster he responded. By the end of the year, Teddy had become one of the brightest students in the class. Despite her lie, he had become one of the "teacher's pets."

A year later, she found a note under the door from Teddy telling her that she was the best teacher he'd ever had in his whole life.

Six years passed by, and to her surprise, another note came from Teddy. He wrote that he had finished high school third in his class and that she was still the best teacher that he'd ever had in his whole life.

Four years later, another letter came, saying that while things had been tough at times, he stayed in school and stuck with it and that he had graduated from college with the highest of honors. He assured Mrs. Thompson that she was still the very best and favorite teacher he'd ever had in his whole life.
Four more years passed by and yet another letter came. This time, he explained that after he got his bachelor's degree, he had decided to go a little further. Again, assuring her that she was still the best and favorite teacher he'd ever had. The letter was signed, Theodore F. Stoddard, MD.

The story doesn't end there. There was one final letter that spring. Teddy said that he had met this girl and that he was going to be married. He explained that his father had died a couple of years prior, and he was wondering if Mrs. Thompson might agree to sit in the place at his wedding that was usually reserved for the mother of the groom. Of course, Mrs. Thompson agreed.

She wore that bracelet, the one with the several rhinestones missing. She also made sure she was wearing the perfume that Teddy remembered his mother wearing on their last Christmas together.

After the wedding, they hugged each other as Dr. Stoddard whispered in Mrs. Thompson's ear, "Thank you so much for making me feel important and showing me that I could make a difference." With tears in her eyes, Mrs. Thompson whispered back, "Teddy, you have it all wrong. You were the one who taught me that I could make a difference. I didn't know how to teach until I met you."

-Author Unknown

This story communicates what teaching and learning are all about. If there is no learning, there is no teaching. I think teachers must take a close look at themselves when evaluating their effectiveness as educators. There is no doubt that most teachers know their content, and they understand it well. Yet, if you're not reaching the student and the student refuses to learn from you, other techniques and strategies must be explored and executed.

Teddy came alive after Mrs. Thompson read his files and identified what he was dealing with outside of school. She began meeting him where he was; Teddy needed compassion and love. I encourage all teachers to get to know their students—all of them.

An experienced educator is acutely aware of their students' learning styles and insecurities, usually within the first couple of months of school. Knowing what makes a student comfortable enough to want to learn is a skill that heightens as experience in the classroom grows.

Questions Teachers Should Ask Themselves:

- Have I reviewed any of my students' past academic records?

- Do I teach any students that I would like to know more about their culture?

- Do I vary my teaching to address different learning styles?

$\Rightarrow$ CHAPTER SIX $\Leftarrow$

Be That Difference

Teachers have always made a difference in the lives of children. Without teachers, knowledge would cease to be transferred from one generation to the next. Teachers advance society by exposing ideas and topics to their students. Because of good teachers, we have good physicians, reasonable attorneys, scientists, and we live in an educated society. Teachers should make a difference in the lives of all their students, regardless of their racial, cultural, or ethnic background.

For most of my teaching career, I have taught students with special needs who happened to be of a different racial experience than myself. This allowed me to bond with students who had preconceived ideas about others who looked like me. Also, I had the opportunity to touch the lives of students that learned differently and was able to make a difference in how they viewed themselves.

Teachers have to be that difference and make a difference. Sometimes students do not have much confidence in their ability to perform academically. Good teachers motivate students to believe in themselves and their academic potential.

I did everything within my power to show that I loved them regardless of any differences that society may have attempted to place upon us. I realized that I could not teach them until I reached them. I had to make them feel comfortable with me as a person before I could expect them to learn from me. In a perfect world, that may not have been needed. But let's face it, we are not perfect; we are human.

We see color, recognize economic status, and observe academic abilities and disabilities. The difference is how we respond to the people that look and learn differently than we do. Although we have these differences, every effort should respect and celebrate our differences. Until we can legitimately internalize this philosophy, we will always fall short of reaching the most disadvantaged students and meeting their educational needs.

Otherwise, we will never help our students reach goals that others have attained. No dream should seem inaccessible to any student that applies himself. They are called teachers to make sure that their students believed this to be true.

The Mental State of Teachers

Most teachers love students, are excellent role models, and want to impact their students positively. Whenever I talk to students that share how I made a difference in their lives, it reinforces why I entered this wonderful profession. Educators, in general, want to make a difference in the lives of their students. Educators are very good at seeing the potential of their students and strive to make students work hard to reach their potential.

At times, educators are falsely accused of not liking students simply because of certain expectations that other educators may not have shared. Moreover, teachers can also experience specific life stressors, such as declining health, burnout, aging parents, or the sudden loss of a spouse or a child, which may appear to be a temporary disconnection from the affective domain of teaching.

There is a need for an outlet for stressed educators, so they can effectively address the stressors in the lives of their students. Sometimes, teachers' vocal tones are perceived as a little harsh because they are concerned. This can easily be misconstrued as the teacher not liking a student. When this is brought to the teacher's attention, I'm confident that most teachers will take the appropriate steps to mitigate the problem and continue to make a difference in the lives of their students.

Administrators Can Make a Difference

Schools usually have a student handbook, which is used as a guide for outlining the rules and regulations for student conduct. Administrators must remember that this is only a guide and should not be used on every occasion or student. There are always exceptions to every rule.

Rules in school are meant to teach students what is acceptable in society in general. Whenever these rules are broken, consequences follow. Sometimes consequences come across as being punitive and can cause students to become emotionally disconnected from school. Giving a student a break can sometimes make a significant difference in their life. It can help build their confidence in the school administration and help them believe that it's okay to make mistakes that are, at times, forgivable.

There were times as an administrator when I deviated from the "rule book" and talked to students to gain their trust and confidence. For so many of them, this was all that was needed to reconnect the emotionally disconnected students back to the school.

Everyone Deserves a Second Chance

It's important to remember that we're not dealing with products on an assembly line that become broken; with products, you have the luxury of throwing out the broken or defective ones. As educators, we have an essential role in preparing lives that may have been broken before meeting them. Nevertheless, we have the tremendous responsibility of helping make them whole again. We have all been broken at one time or another during our lifetime, but someone decided to give us another chance.

Remember, teachers and administrators are called to make a difference in their students!

My wife and I were sitting on a plane one afternoon, about to leave Philadelphia for San Antonio, Texas, when a tall, handsome young man came down the aisle. He stopped in front of us and said:

"Mr. Bland, I don't know if you remember me, but I am Jim. You asked me to come to your room one day during your prep period. You talked to me for the entire period about life and the importance of getting an education. You didn't know then, but I had planned to drop out of school that year. I stayed in school, graduated, and now I am on my way to basic training for the United States Air Force."

I had no idea that he was contemplating dropping out of school. Although I had forgotten the conversation, he hadn't, and it made a difference in his life.

The Starfish Story by Loren Eiseley has always inspired me as an educator. It goes like this:

An old man was walking on the beach one morning after a storm. In the distance, he could see someone moving like a dancer. As he came closer, he saw that it was a young woman picking up starfish and throwing them into the ocean.

"Young lady, why are you throwing starfish into the ocean?"
"The sun is up, and the tide is going out, and if I do not throw them in, they will die," she said.

"But young lady, do you not realize that there are thousands of starfish? You cannot possibly make a difference."
The young woman listened politely, then bent down, picked up another starfish, and threw it into the sea. "It made a difference for that one."

Most students appreciate teachers going beyond the call of duty, such as attending athletic events of their students. A difference can be made by meeting the student in the hall with a smile, eating lunch with them in the school cafeteria. There are little acts like these that the students will never forget. When your students start to see you as a caring human being, you've reached them, and now it's time to teach them. When they know how much you care, then and only then will they care how much you know.

I wasn't taught at the university to take time out of my planning period to encourage students. Teachers have the tall order of changing lives, and the calling to change lives brings out teachers. Teachers have been called to make a difference! You have been called to make a difference in the lives of your students. You will motivate, inspire, and encourage hundreds of students just by showing up and dispensing knowledge daily. However, if you love them, you will get to know them as a person. The difference is when students are persuaded that you don't just like them, but you love them.

Questions Teachers Should Ask Themselves:

- How can I make a difference in the lives of my students?

- Do I allow my students room for youthful mistakes?

- Do my students believe that I care about them as a person?

⮞ CHAPTER SEVEN ⮜

Home & School Communication

The long-term dangers of a separation between the school and home enlarge the emotional gap between the two. This can have devastating effects on low social-economic and minority families. The lack of communication between the home and school can further hurt students who feel detached from their teachers or peers.

Some parents believe the educational system is an insidious institution to keep them within a particular class. This is an overall contention among many minorities and impoverished families.

Consequently, when their children tell them that a teacher or an administrator doesn't like them, they are more likely to believe them.

As a parent, I can't tell you how many times I've heard my child, as well as other students, rant out the words, "My teacher doesn't like me." I wanted to know the real reasons why. As a parent, I wanted to know the real reasons my child was not performing in a particular class.

I knew there was a problem, and my child was not happy. Parents know when their children aren't as excited about school or about a particular teacher's class. When this occurred with my child, it was a very stressful time in my household.

As parents, we go to work every day to provide for our families, and we want our children to attend school to learn and return home happy. When this doesn't happen, it induces stress upon the whole family. When the excitement of going to school dissipated, I knew I had to meet with the teacher to get to the bottom of the problem. I understood the importance of communicating how my child felt about the class to the teacher. I suspected the teacher didn't know, in totality, what my child was going through in their class.

Some children are intimidated and believe that if they speak to their teachers with the same emotion, it might negatively impact them. Teachers and parents must establish a rapport where the student believes that everyone involved loves them and wants to see them succeed. If not, the student may feel that all the school personnel are insensitive and not particularly interested in their welfare. This can be a complex emotional state for any student and could quite possibly lead to an abundance of harmful activities outside of school.

I'm not suggesting that you call the teacher on the first failed test but certainly do if there's a second and third one. Teachers should reach out to parents when they believe a student is struggling academically to seek more information that may help with instructional delivery. Let me preface this by saying that it is the teacher's responsibility to make the initial contact with the parent. If the teacher fails to contact the parent, you must contact the teacher to save your child. This is a golden opportunity for vital information to be shared between the teacher and the parent.

The teacher has the opportunity to get enlightened by the parent about their child's behavior at home.

Also, the parent has the opportunity to hear if there are any changes in their child's behavior at school. For instance, they should know if their child has recently changed friends while at school or has become indifferent about learning in the classroom.

How Parents Can Identify Detachment

Losing old friends or becoming emotionally disconnected from your fellow students is more prevalent among secondary school children than among those in elementary school.

Unfortunately, most parents do not learn this information from their children. Nevertheless, if there is a drastic change in behavior that is affecting the student's academic performance, it is more than likely that their behavior at home has changed as well.

Parents and teachers must always keep the door of communication open. In my experience, parents are more hands-on with their elementary school children and tend not to communicate as much with teachers in secondary school. For those reasons alone, teachers should contact the parents when the student seems to be less interested in school.

As a result, there can be adjustment periods for secondary school students. Subjects become more specialized and coupled with rigor. Sometimes, this can be challenging for students to navigate through. Therefore, more attention from parents is required to keep their child (ren) focused. Secondary school students also gain exposure to an array of extracurricular activities, which may encourage them to develop new interests.

Moreover, elementary teachers have traditionally had more expectations of their students than secondary teachers, simply due to the fact that the students are still excited about learning. In addition, parental involvement tends to be expected more so from the parents of elementary students than secondary students.

Secondary school teachers also tend to be more content-driven and have less patience for students who are not academically self-propelled. At the same time, parents of secondary school students tend to be more hands-off, for they fear that their child may resent them or that their involvement may make the student appear more sheltered.

As a secondary teacher, I often held meetings with parents who were in a state of confusion as to why their newly promoted secondary school-aged child was no longer interested in academics and did not want them involved in his/her school matters. This is a crucial time in the life of secondary school students; which makes home and school communications critical.

Students often begin working during this time, and the proper integration of their economic, social, and academic worlds can be an arduous task for teenagers. It can become overwhelming and imbalanced, leaving academics on the back burner and the student concluding, "My teacher doesn't like me."

Questions Teachers Should Ask Parentsat the Start of the Year:

- What are your concerns about your child this school year?

- How and when would you like me to communicate with you this year?

- Is there anything you can tell me about your child that may help me support their learning?

CHAPTER EIGHT

Teacher Values

Teachers are expected to be role models in society; they should represent fairness for all students. I suppose this is why so many strict rules were placed on teachers in the 1800s. At one time in America, teachers and ministers were two of the most respected professions in our society

Society recognizes that children spend a significant amount of time with teachers, and it is essential that they set good examples as law-abiding citizens. Although I'm afraid I disagree with many of the rules set in that era, I believe teachers must have a code of ethics.

Moreover, the teacher certification board recognizes the significance of a teacher's image and how much of an influence we have on our students and the parents, and the community as a whole. Parents want to believe that their children are being taught and influenced by good, honest, and loving human beings.

The textbooks for teacher-education programs contend that teachers are not to teach values. I agree with this but only to a certain extent. There are some values such as honesty, respect, bravery, and fairness that should be taught and exhibited by teachers daily, as they are supposed to be the role models. When our students see these values in their teachers, they will be more likely to trust them. This opens the door for student/teacher trust to reach new heights.

Similarly, when a student believes a teacher cares about their welfare, they try harder to be successful in the classroom and school overall. Trust, respect, and honesty will teach the children how to conduct themselves among their peers.

As an administrator, I was once confronted with a situation that tested my advocacy for students. I received a phone call from one of my superiors that tested my core values.

At the time, we had a rule in place that any student

who had accumulated a certain number absences would be excluded from the graduation ceremony. I had one student who was the child of a school board member who fell within this category. My superior phoned me and instructed me to allow this student to participate in the graduation ceremonydespite his many unexcused absences. Of course, I had to comply because he was my boss.

It bothered me that many other students would not participate in the graduation ceremony because of their unexcused absences. This conflicted with my core values, and I was troubled within. I asked my secretary to pull up every student excluded from the ceremony because of unexcused absences and make appointments for each student to meet with me. I then informed all the students that they would participate in the graduation ceremony.

The student who was allowed to graduate because his father was a school board member was given special privileges, and I was totally against this kind of inequity. Had I not chosen to make that decision, those students who were prohibited from attending the graduating ceremonies would have been justified in concluding, "My principal doesn't like me."

Students who do not have parents or the proper connections to obtain advocates should not be penalized. I've always attempted to level the playing field for all students while being an example of fairness and equity for all. No student should ever feel as though they are irrelevant because of a lack of advocacy. It is the same way ordinary people feel when they experience injustice because of their lack of advocacy.

Economics and social status, just as race or gender, should never be a determining factor for a student to receive equal treatment. When students experience overt inequalities, they will always adopt the mindset, "my teacher, school, or principal doesn't like me." Students and parents are not blind to social injustices that occur in schools.

Regarding Family Values

Educators should refrain from using the one-size-fits-all approach to impart values to students. We must respect cultural differences and family values while helping children turn into socially responsible and successful adults.

There is no denying that the idea of teaching values to students may seem subjective to some. However, just like how parents take extra care to ensure their child is aware of their specific family values, teachers must also model and reinforce positive behavior in the classroom.

We are responsible for shaping the young minds that spend a significant part of their day with us. Therefore, we must take every measure to ensure they are prepared to take on the challenges of the real world.

Developing Core Values

Kindness is one of the core values that educators can help develop in their students through classroom activities. If teachers show acts of kindness and compassion to their students and their colleagues, the children are likely to model the behavior.

Empathy also goes hand in hand with kindness. It encourages young individuals to look after each other and gain a deeper understanding of human emotions. This way, if a particular student is struggling with anxiety in the classroom or has begun to show signs of emotional detachment, their peers may be able to figure out what's wrong and help them get back on track.

Furthermore, teachers can encourage students to become more honest by telling them it is okay to make mistakes. Once children realize that they won't be punished or reprimanded, they will become more likely to own up to their mistakes.

As educators, we must also create environments that reinforce positive value systems and develop the core values of responsibility, compassion, patience, self-discipline, acceptance, integrity, respect for others, and willingness to compromise. Learning these values will help students from different socioeconomic, ethnic, and religious backgrounds develop a harmonious relationship both inside and outside of the school.

Questions Teachers Should Ask Themselves:

- What values am I modeling for my students?

- What values should I focus on instilling in my students?

- What thought-provoking questions should I ask my students about core values?

CHAPTER NINE

The Indifferent Learner

In this chapter, I will discuss various categories of indifferent learners and suggest ways to reach them. I hope academic barriers will be removed and the overall learning experience will be optimized.

When educators know the kind of students that sit in front of them, they can establish an environment that breeds learning. One of the most difficult students to reach is the shy and withdrawn student. Other types of students who may seem disinterested in class may be the abused student, the minority student, the impoverished student, and the disruptive student.

The Introvert/Shy Student

In school, I gravitated to one or two other people whom I called my friends. I never liked to hang out with large crowds, even today. The shy and introverted student is often misunderstood because of the minimal verbal interactions with their peers and teachers. However, being shy is no indication of their mental aptitude. Some people have concluded that if you're not socially integrated into many activities in school, something is wrong.

Although I'm not negating this, it is risky to assume without probing. Perhaps a student has to work after school to help support the family financially, or maybe the parents are divorced. The student spends time as a caretaker for younger siblings, which precludes them from participating in certain activities. Why are they always alone? Sometimes students prefer not to have many friends.

I always sought to integrate students who appeared to isolate themselves. I encouraged the shy child to lead a discussion on a subject that they were passionate about and knew more about than their peers. This is a great strategy I used to help build a student's self-confidence. I've always gravitated to the shy students.

As a teacher, I wanted to find out what made them tick. I knew that if I could genuinely befriend them and gain their trust as a teacher; I could get them to learn. I wanted to place them in an emotionally safe environment where they could flourish. Behind these shy individuals, I found lovely students who were very eager to learn, and teaching them was even more enjoyable. What often happens is that many tend to draw inaccurate conclusions. This, the shy and withdrawnstudents may believe no one likes them, including their teachers. Some students become withdrawn because no one has ever approached them to join them or hang out with them.

Meanwhile, some teachers are content-driven and do not have time to make small talk with their students. We must be careful not to label those teachers as not liking their students, just as some people are labeled as being conceited because they don't mix with many people.

The problem sometimes occurs when inflammatory remarks are made and inappropriate behavior becomes the result.

Often, shy students are labeled as not being academically capable or not as "smart," as their outgoing peers. The fact is, some students are just not as outgoing as other students. When I was in school, I found myself being more attracted to only afew people rather than a crowd. I believe this is a person's prerogative and should be respected. I believe it happens with teachers and with students as well. But I do not believe that it should result in being mistreated or placed in a category of misfits. When this bleeds over into the mind of an educator, it can be emotionally lethal.

I've heard some students being called "weird" because they were introverts when in actuality they might have been excommunicated by their peers. Silence does not mean one is ignorant or unmotivated to learn.

Some shy students lack the coping skills to address situational demands. Teachers must endeavor to win shy students' confidence while reassuring them that they are emotionally safe when around them. When this is accomplished, you are sure to find an attractive young man or woman who will enrich your life, just as Teddy Stoddard did for Mrs. Thompson.

The Abused Student

Another type of indifferent learner that educators may encounter is the abused student.

Abuse can range from mental to physical and involve many different levels. Students who are abused sometimes become loners for fear that someone may find out about their situation. Physical abuse is noticed more often as it is easier to see, but the subtle signs of mental abuse can be just as devastating. Teachers should work cooperatively with guidance counselors and other school agencies to ensure that a safe environment is engineered and maintained to maximize learning.

Mental abuse should never occur in a classroom. When a student becomes withdrawn, the appropriate staff should get involved to help them. If the student is only withdrawn while in school, the teacher should contact the parents and seek more information about the situation. The details shared by the parents can help the teacher find ways to engage the student. A meeting with the administration is advised so the jurisdictional lines are not crossed and confidentiality is not breached.

The Underprivileged Student

The impoverished or economically challenged students also deal with a whole new set of challenges that are often hard to conceptualize unless you have lived in their shoes.

One of the most outstanding books I've ever read was by an American educator and author, Dr. Ruby Payne. Her book on understanding poverty as it relates to education enlightened me immensely.

I knew how to remediate students of certain concepts academically, but how do you get students to do their homework when they don't have a home? How do you meet with parents to discuss their child's academic progression or regression during your work hours when there is only one parent in the home and that sole provider cannot take a day off work for fear of losing a day's pay?

The impoverished student often hides his academic deficiencies; just as he does his poverty. Because of poverty, many students miss out on opportunities and are often overlooked. In some cases, impoverished students may believe that their teacher doesn't like them. Students should not suffer academically because they are deprived economically. Some programs will assist with tutoring, the buying of computers, etc.

The Withdrawn Student

Another category of indifferent learner is the withdrawn student.

Students can become withdrawn for several reasons, just like Teddy. However, indifferent attitudes toward learning typically occur over a period of time. Hence, teachers must investigate and seek to discover the reasons a student may have adopted a nonchalant attitude toward learning. You will often find bright students with excellent academic potential feeling emotionally disconnected from their surroundings.

My aloofness toward school in the seventh grade resulted from being placed in an environment that was racially foreign to me. Consequently, I was left in a state of culture shock. Some students become withdrawn because they don't have much success academically and settle to keep to themselves rather than exposing their academic deficiencies to their peers.

Other withdrawn students may come from dysfunctional homes. The social skills of such children tend to be highly radical or remain in a state of paralysis. Whatever the reason, a concerned teacher will investigate and develop a plan to properly reach the student so that learning occurs.

The Disruptive Student

Easily distracted students are often noticeably academically deficient or academically talented. Their attention span is usually short, which causes them to stay off task, resulting in them becoming disruptive in class. Our curriculum usually does not accommodate this type of student within the regular classroom setting. If the student is given a task that is more rigorous, initially they may resist and become even more disruptive.

This type of student must have a parent meeting immediately. Past academic performance must be extracted from the school records, and the guidance department should be involved in every meeting. If the disruptive student is exceedingly academically talented, the same meeting with parental involvement with the guidance counselor should take place. Another academic setting with more rigor may result in the students' disruption subsiding.

The other kind of disruptive student is the student that may struggle with certain concepts. This student uses being a disruption to divert attention from their own deficiencies.

Careful planning to remediate this kind of student and building an educational plan to remediate unlearned concepts can quickly restore confidence and give the student another way of receiving attention. Attention is usually what the disruptive students yearn for. Unfortunately, they have not learned the best way to get raw attention. A behavior modification plan should be put in place to help such students obtain the appropriate attention that he or she is so badly trying to seek

The plan should allow the behavior to be easily obtainable and monitored in short time intervals. As time progresses, the duration should be lengthened. In addition, it is always important to give praise for appropriate behavior. As one of my professors said; "Notice the good, and the bad will get better."

The Minority Student

Sometimes, minority students may be misunderstood as being indifferent learners. As a result of this misunderstanding, they may also believe their teacher doesn't like them because they don't look like other students in the classroom. Prejudging anyone or anything is a great disservice and can affect a child's life for many years. Every student that sits in your classroom deserves an opportunity to learn, regardless of how they look on the outside. Educators can unlock academic doors that have been closed due to years of prejudgment.

Many of life's most valued treasures have been overlooked and passed up in students because someone didn't take the time to discover why they were underperforming and what made them tick. Thus, many have been unduly relegated to certain places or positions. Many opportunities for students have been missed because of their outward appearance and because of prejudgment.

Unfortunately, we live in a society where this is too often the case and is commonplace. No one's race, nationality, ethnicity, gender, or religion should ever be a deciding factor of their abilities or capabilities.

Whenever the classroom door swings open, it should symbolize limitless opportunities for every student who enters. Most parents genuinely believe that opportunities are gained through obtaining an education. It is rare for a parent to believe that their child, or children, may be given less of an opportunity than the next child simply because they look different.

Therefore, it is incumbent upon all educators to make sure that these opportunities are afforded to every student. During the Jim Crow Era, under the Separate but Equal law, the educational inequities between Blacks and the schools for Whites were widely known. However, nothing was accomplished to abolish them until it went to the Supreme Court in Brown vs. Topeka Board of Education.

Sadly, the inequalities still exist due to what I refer to as "classroom segregation." I've seen some teachers give two different spelling lists because they believed the students were spelling on two different levels and that some students weren't capable of being as successful at specific tasks as others. Please don't misunderstand me; I understand that all students are not always similar. But what objective indices are you using to determine such tracking?

When my daughter was in elementary school, she came home with a spelling list that appeared to be below her grade level. When my wife and I inquired about it, she stated, "Oh, I have the easy list. There is another list that the smart students get." Well, needless to say, I met with the teacher to ask what qualifications she utilized to determine group placement for each spelling test. She informed me that it was a pretest that she'd administered at the beginning of the year. This was unacceptable to me. Hence, I insisted on my daughter being placed in a group that received on-level spelling words. My daughter never made less than an "A" on her spelling test for the rest of the year. I'm not against grouping, but I'm totally against not giving everyone an equal opportunity to rise to the challenge.

My undergraduate degree is in Special Education, and my professors instructed me that I should always teach my students in such a manner that it looks like I'm trying to put myself out of a job.

There are some school districts that have set up gate-keeping mechanisms to weed out certain students, preventing them from enrolling in specific courses that reflect a rigorous curriculum.

This should never be part of determining if any student has the opportunity to get an education, regardless of what they look like, their accent, or their economic status. Parents and students need to know that the school offers a level playing field when it comes to having the same opportunities as their counterparts.

Verbalizing this to your students isn't enough until it is exhibited in front of them. With that being said, it is not until we have the opportunity to interact with each other that we can find the natural treasures of knowing one another. Many students have concluded that their teacher doesn't like them because the communication between the teacher and the student is invariably superficial.

Questions Teachers Should Ask Themselves:

- Do any of my students appear Indifferent toward learning?

- What can I do to engage socially isolated students?

- Have I contacted parents to get more information on my indifferent learners?

$\Rightarrow$ CONCLUSION $\Leftarrow$

As a teacher, you have been given a special gift to help shape and change the lives of all people, both young and old, men and women. Some of my most gratifying experiences have been when I've heard that some of my "at-risk" students have gone on to accept prominent positions in education.

As mentioned in Chapter One, I believe teaching is a calling. Teaching requires a love for the profession and especially a love for children. I've had students I did not like; that is, I wouldn't say I wanted certain behaviors they may have exhibited, but I loved them. I loved them enough to reach out and conference with them and their parents. I loved them enough not to give up on them. I did not always "like" my own children, that is, their behavior, but I've always loved them.

It is very easy to see when a teacher loves what they do. It is even more evident to see when a teacher loves their students. A teacher who loves their students will go the extra mile to ensure they are learning and that their classroom is a safe haven for all of them.

Schools provide services to a variety of students with various needs, and it is our responsibility to use whatever special services, techniques, and methods necessary to make the withdrawn student feel wanted and loved regardless of their outward appearance or economic status. As teachers, we have been chosen to touch the future by ensuring that every student who sits in front of us maximizes all of their capabilities, thereby becoming a contributing member of society.

In the teaching profession, we are blessed to work with people. We have been given the opportunity to help shape someone's personality and future.

I honestly cannot think of one student whom I did not like as a person. There were many times that I did not particularly like their behavior that was being exhibited, and it may have been a bit more challenging to manage it in some instances. Still, I found a way to gain the confidence of my students by making them feel safe in my classroom.

I had to show students that I was not against them because of the way they looked or because of their parents' economic status. I had to show them that I loved them and wanted to see them succeed. I wanted each student to believe that they were a valued member of my class.

Sometimes it is a feat to persuade a child that you accept and love them, regardless of their past. Keep in mind; some students may have never had anyone say anything positive to them. So, they enter your classroom with a negative perception of themselves. It's not easy, but true love for your students has the power to change any student.

As educators, we must remember that we hold the key to unlocking and maximizing each student's learning potential in the classroom. We must assist these young individuals in developing positive relationships with others based on trust and honesty, believing that they will carry these values on with them throughout their lifetime.

Though it may be challenging and require a lot of patience, teachers must also strive to build a meaningful and respectful relationship with their students. Learning more about their students also helps educators establish content relevance to nurture impressionable minds and foster academic success.

If your students can see you making an effort to reach out to them, there is a good chance they will reciprocate. As your bond strengthens, your students will finally realize that the voice inside their head reminding them, "My teacher doesn't like me," was indeed wrong.

LETTERS FROM
FORMER STUDENTS

Jennifer Simkanen

22 years later and I still hold such love, admiration and appreciation for Dr. Bland.

I was badly bullied throughout my high school years. I would hide in every janitor closet, bathroom, and school corner to avoid altercations in the hallways.

I started cutting school, considered suicide, and constantly felt alone and like I didn't belong. I filled a void with a very abusive relationship that left me unexpectedly pregnant during my senior year and the only option I saw to protect myself and my unborn child was dropping out.

My mother, feeling completely helpless and heartbroken, reached out to Dr. Bland - who was the principal in the grade below mine. Dr. Bland was immediately responsive, caring, and compassionate. He saw a higher version of myself than I was able to see, and in that reflection, I was able to begin believing in myself again.

He provided me with a sense of safety and belonging and gave me the dignity to walk my high school halls without fear.

Still to this day, I consider him my Hero. He saved me when I didn't believe I was worth saving. The love and compassion he showed me allowed me to grow into the strong and compassionate woman I continue be today – a woman who, raised two beautiful daughters on her own, instilling such love and morals, who beat cancer at age 24, and who, at the age of 25, held her mom's hand while she died from a brain tumor.

I'm a certified yoga instructor who teaches mindfulness. I have my skydiving license with 77 jumps under my wings, and am the matriarch of a beautiful blended family of five children. Every beautiful soul I encounter daily, from all walks of life, I always give back what Dr. Bland gave to me – compassion and worth.

Dr. Bland, I am so deeply grateful for you and I know I'm not the only one. You see the greatness and potential in everyone you meet and have an innate way of leading people back to their worth and wholeness. This book will no doubt help others to understand the utmost shift that can happen when we learn to love without discrimination in connection with our hearts and our integrity.

Believing in someone ignites and fuels the doubts we all struggle with and creates space to believe in thyself.

Gratefully,
Jennifer Simkanin

Jennifer Simkanin, her daughter,
my wife, and me

Andrea McCollick:

In 1990, a seventh-grade girl was simply walking down the hallway, smiling to approach her friends at their lockers. Out of nowhere, a rather tall man, wearing brightly colored Zubaz, approached me. He simply stated that I was always smiling, and he wondered why and asked my name. That moment started a friendship that impacted every adult choice I ever made. I call it the "Bland Trickle Effect" or the BTE.

His impact on students within his classroom walls and outside his classroom walls inspired me to venture into the education field. Every interview I had ever been on, I was asked why I wanted to be a special education teacher. My answer was always simply, "Dr. Bland at Neshaminy Jr. High School empowered me to want to see the good in others and teach them to see the good in themselves."

He showed compassion, respect and a desire to connect to others in order for them to feel safe within his classroom environment. These qualities have helped me hone in on my craft of being a special education teacher and also a case manager for students with special needs. I am forever grateful for being a part of the "BTE."

Jamie Ilene Schwartz Kaelin:
It was 1995 my senior year in high school...I should have graduated in 1994 but GOD had other plans. I was blessed to cross paths with an extraordinary human with class and kindness that permeated out of his soul...It's like when he smiled at you, your whole day got brighter.

Let me introduce Mr. Bland...to describe how he influenced my life would take a novel of my own, but here's the brief version. Most people associate high school with popularity, sports, homecoming, student council etc. What stood out to me was Mr. Bland.

As I struggled with being bullied and adulthood (at that age) he reminded me to keep smiling and that being unique is special and that we all have a purpose in this world. At that age it was nice to feel appreciated and accepted (even if it wasn't from your peers).

He was like the reverend of Neshaminy High School. He taught us equality. I got way more than an education. It's the way he taught us...his demeanor was calm and soothing; a total peacemaker, and so non-judgmental with our decisions in life whether school or personal. He was so there and not because he had to but because he genuinely wanted to...we all felt that way.

Till this day one story stands out...it was our last senior event and we were on The Spirit of

Philadelphia and thanks to him, not only was I accepted by him but my peers too. I was able to interact with other students and smile just as bright as he would in those halls. That was our final goodbye.

My name is Jamie Ilene Schwartz Kaelin and at 44 years I have never encountered such an influential, classy, giving, hardworking and family-oriented man who, when it comes to providing his students an education, it's truly magical what transpires at 18 years old. So thank you for your wisdom, and for showing us the power of smiling. Not only can it make your day itcan make someone else's.

To say I am blessed to have you as my friend and the most influential person in my life is an understatement. I am honored Mr. Bland, to know such a beautiful person. I love you for teaching me to love myself.

Kia Adams:
I was privileged enough to encounter Dr. Bland more than once in my life. Our first encounter, though

indirect, gave me a great sense of how much he valued instilling education in others. He tutored my brother when he was ill; mostly in math and he was even nice enough to allow me to engage and even threw some math questions my way as well.

He always managed to put a smile on my brothers' face and not only made learning fun, but a priority to him. My brother had been diagnosed with a rare cancer at the age of 15 and his chance of remission was not likely. I always remembered Dr. Bland making it a priority to come see my brother and I believe him coming to tutor and just give his time gave my brother hope to fight.

Sometimes people just need someone to have faith and hope when they don't have it themselves and Dr. Bland gave that to my brother and our family. Although my brother passed in 1994 Dr. Bland always continued to check on myself and the rest of my family.

Jennifer Conrad:

Dr. Bland is the type of person who uplifts you. He gives you confidence even when you're having a bad day. He always listened without judgment; and understood me even if he didn't agree. He taught me to never stop being true to who I am. His positive impact on my life will never be forgotten. I am forever grateful for crossing paths with him.

Pictured here is a former student, JenniferConrad Johnson, her husband Keyshawn Johnson and their family along with somemembers of my family

Debbie Stern:

Dr. Bland; my all-time favorite person at Neshaminy! How are you? I have an interesting story for you! I live in Lancaster and work for Hospice. I am the "night nurse" I was at a time of death visit and called a funeral home in Coatesville. When the gentleman arrived to take the body I said, "Wow, you remind me of my principal in high school!" The gentleman said I hope that's a good thing, to which I told him it was a wonderful thing. After we got the body into the van they came back and said we don't just take the loved one we like to have prayer. We held hands and all prayed. I commented on how much that meant to the family and to myself. The kind man then said, "Are you talking about Dr. Bland?  I was blown away.

1. Thank you for the lifelong impression you left on my heart.

2. Thank you for your love for God, people, and being God's messenger. I hope you know just how amazing you are and the lives you have impacted .

Christopher Benwah Bennett:

Long ago...20 years perhaps; you changed my life. The 1st person in my life that showed me REAL respect as a teenager was my highly educated black school principal. Although I understand you may not remember me, I have never forgotten the wisdom you gave me 20 years ago while sitting in your office. I actually believe it was the last time I got in trouble at school and it changed my whole mentality in 11th grade...even to this day.

INSTEAD of calling my parents, which was the usual thing when I got in trouble...you were about to call them and then looked at me .....then I'm not sure what clicked in your head but you sighed and then told me that you weren't going to call them.

Then you talked to me for a good 1.5 hrs about my life decisions. About the choices in life that I didn't even know existed. After I walked out of the office above the library, my life changed immediately.

Hope, Respect, Perseverance

Virginia Ingram:

As an emancipated minor, living in a group home through most of my high school years, YOU made an unbelievably positive impact on my life & future. Thank you for showing me stern kindness and understanding during the hardest time of my life. I still tell the story... I got sent to the principal's office so many times during my English class. Eventually, Dr. Bland decided to just give me a job there in the office... 😄 true story! I hope your life is as wonderful as you deserve.

Sincerely,
Virginia Ingram
Class of 2001

Chuck Kanian:

I don't know if you remember me Dr. Bland, but you are the reason I became a social worker. You guided me and when I needed you, you helped me become better. I was not a bad kid in high school but I was entering into a bad spot of criminality. If you and my parents did not stop and care for me, I would be in jail. You are the man and great job with the new profession. I have since left social work but you were the reason I went into it. I helped so many kids. God bless sir!

A Special Letter Written to My Father by a Former Student, After His Death.

MY TRIBUTE TO A GREAT TEACHER:
There are some amazing people who touch your life who you will never forget. At six I started school. My teacher's name was Miss Thompson. She taught 1st through 5th grade in a one room school. After the first day I knew I wanted to be a teacher. Years later, walking into my freshmen English class, there was this man talking about the eight parts of speech. It was so confusing! Then he began to diagram sentences. Wow!! My world burst into sunshine and I was hooked. I fell in love with words.

Mr. Edgar Bland was my amazing English teacher and was the motivation for my decision to become a high school English teacher. I taught for twenty-eight years and never without thanking God for these two wonderful teachers who loved their craft and children.

Mr. Bland, in my eyes was a big, robust man with eyes that lit up when he was in class. He pushed us until we got it. He didn't play, but I knew he loved us. Thank you to his wife and sons, Percy Bland Sr. and Vandell Bland, for sharing your love for this great man and for the memories of my favorite teacher. I love my teacher still and my prayer is that he will continue to Rest in Love in the arms of Jesus. Gone but I will never ever forget him!!! Thank you Mr Bland!!!

Corine Allen

MEANINGFUL

PHOTOGRAPHS

Me in my classroom,
Neshaminy High School in
1995

My wife, Dr. LaFaye
Bland, Neshaminy High

Me in my office at Neshaminy High School

Features

December 23, 1994   page 2

Teacher of the issue:

Mr. Bland supports individual needs of students

Dave Lowing and Brian Aron
Staff Writers

The teaching philosophy of English teacher Mr. Bland is simple, he treats every student as an individual. "I'm here to use special services of methods that I have acquired to assure each student develops to their own capabilities. I want to ensure that they become a contributor to society rather than one who extracts from society," says Mr. Bland, currently in his tenth year at Neshaminy. He believes in establishing a strong relationship with his students. Students learn better when there is a real personal teaching them."

Almost as unique as his teaching philosophy is his background. Mr. Bland grew up in Arkansas, where he was a local high school basketball star. After graduation, Bland attended Arkansas State University. He received his bachelors degree in 1979 followed

by his masters in 1980. Mr. Bland began his teaching career in Arkansas, where he spent five years, before moving to this area. In addition to being an English teacher, he is certified in Secondary Administration.

Mr. Bland's diverse hobbies include traveling and basketball, as well as just sitting by the pool and reading. Among the various books he's read, Mr. Bland especially enjoys the work of Maya Angelou. Ms. Angelou is a renowned poet and writer who read one of her poems at President Clinton's inauguration. Once he gets started reading one of her works, Mr. Bland says that he finds it hard to put it down.

The Bland family resides in Chadds Ford, about fifty miles away. The family includes Mrs. Bland, who teaches at Neshaminy in the business department, a son and two daughters. Mr. Bland believes in a strong central family so he is very close with them. Mr. Bland has dedicated himself to other people as

Despite the fifty mile commute, he is a former basketball coach at Neshaminy Jr. High School and is the pastor of the "Pentecostal House of Prayer." Mr. Bland has done evangelistic work in twenty-five different states with his church.

When asked why he travels fifty miles to and from Neshaminy, he said, "I like Neshaminy a lot and don't mind it [the commute] either, teaching is what I do, and I like what I do."

When asked what his favorite thing about teaching at Neshaminy High School is, he responded "My favorite thing about Neshaminy is the personal relationship that develops with my students, it's a very special feeling."

English teacher Mr. Bland towers over cameraman, blackboard and classroom alike

**1994 School Newspaper,
"Teacher of the Year Issue"**

**Ginny and I at a
Neshaminy High School
prom**

**My daughter, Attorney Kelly
Adams;teaching one of her
college classes**

My daughter, Raea Wilson, a 5thgrade elementary teacher in Howard County, Maryland

My grandmother, Miriam Nero Edmonson, sharesa moment with an enthusiastic student at ElaineIndustrial School

My senior picture at Central High School in Helena, Arkansas. I am 15years old here

My father, retired educator, Edgar Bland, Sr.

With my brother, Dr. Byron Bland, Sr., in 2007 after receiving his Doctorate

My Doctoral Advisor, Sister Anne Marie Burton

Me sitting in the front of the wagon on the
Elaine Industrial School Campus. Also pictured
is my older brother Vandell, my uncle James and
two aunts; Miriam and Veronica. Literally, some
of the best years of my life!

Made in the USA
Las Vegas, NV
24 March 2022